ESSENTIAL

Wok & Stir-Fry

Contents

Introduction

Almost all Oriental cookery requires the use of a wok. If you have one then an expansive array of wonderful dishes are open to you. There are many different types of woks and they come in various sizes. They are generally made from either stainless steel, cast iron or copper. If you are buying a new wok then a cast iron one is the best choice as this type of wok retains heat the most effectively. The most appropriate size for the average family is approximately 30–35 cm/ 12–14 inches.

There are numerous advantages to cooking with a wok rather than a frying pan. Firstly, the convex shape allows the food to move with ease when stirring or tossing which enables the food to cook much more quickly. As the wok also has curved sides, the heat rises and the whole wok becomes a hot cooking surface, therefore conserving fuel.

The wok is most widely used for stir-frying, a technique which originated in China and which continues to remain the most recognised form of cooking throughout most of South East Asia. In China it is called *Ch'au* which means stirring one or a selection of thinly sliced ingredients evenly in a little hot oil while stirring with long bamboo chopsticks or a spatula.

A common method of stir-frying is by cooking food in batches. This allows ingredients with longer cooking times to be stir-fried first. Once the first batch of ingredients have been cooked, they should be removed from the pan to be returned at a later stage. The dish is always brought together at the end of cooking in the wok and served as a whole. By using this method the required textures for individual ingredients can be easily obtained whilst combining various distinctive flavours.

Across the Far East woks are used in various guises. There is the Indian *karahi*, a wok-like vessel used to make the infamous curry named after the pan. In Indonesia there is the *wajan* used to cook curries, rice dishes and stir-fries. Indeed, the same applies in Japan, Thailand, Singapore and Malaysia, all of which have been influenced by Chinese cooking.

The wok and the stir-frying method of cooking is essential to Asian and Far Eastern cooking, being swift, light, healthy and extremely versatile. The recipes in this book will be sure to take you on a magical journey of the Far East.

Spicy Chicken Noodle Soup

Serves 4

INGREDIENTS

2 tbsp tamarind paste
4 red Thai chillies, finely chopped
2 cloves garlic, crushed
2.5 cm/1-inch piece Thai ginger, peeled and very finely chopped
4 tbsp fish sauce
2 tbsp palm sugar or caster (superfine) sugar
8 lime leaves, roughly torn
1.2 litres/2 pints/5 cups chicken stock
350 g/12 oz boneless chicken breast
100 g/3½ oz carrots, very thinly sliced
350 g/12 oz sweet potato, diced
100 g/3½ oz baby corn cobs, halved
3 tbsp fresh coriander (cilantro), roughly chopped
100 g/3½ oz cherry tomatoes, halved
150 g/5½ oz flat rice noodles
fresh coriander (cilantro), chopped,to garnish

1 Place the tamarind paste, Thai chillies, garlic, Thai ginger, fish sauce, sugar, lime leaves and chicken stock in a large preheated wok and bring to the boil, stirring constantly. Reduce the heat and cook for about 5 minutes.

2 Using a sharp knife, thinly slice the chicken. Add the chicken to the wok and cook for a further 5 minutes, stirring the mixture well.

3 Reduce the heat and add the carrots, sweet potato and baby corn cobs to the wok. Leave to simmer, uncovered, for 5 minutes, or until the vegetables are just tender and the chicken is completely cooked through.

4 Stir in the coriander (cilantro), cherry tomatoes and noodles. Leave the soup to simmer for about 5 minutes, or until the noodles are tender. Garnish and serve hot.

COOK'S TIP

Tamarind paste is produced from the seed pod of the tamarind tree. It adds both a brown colour and tang to soups and gravies. If unavailable, dilute molasses (dark muscovado) sugar or treacle with lime juice.

Spicy Thai Soup with Prawns (Shrimp)

Serves 4

INGREDIENTS

2 tbsp tamarind paste
4 red Thai chilies, very finely chopped
2 cloves garlic, crushed
2.5 cm/1 inch piece Thai ginger, peeled and very finely chopped
4 tbsp fish sauce
2 tbsp palm sugar or caster (superfine) sugar
8 lime leaves, roughly torn
1.2 litres/2 pints/5 cups fish stock
100 g/3½ oz carrots, very thinly sliced
350 g/12 oz sweet potato, diced
100 g/3½ oz/1 cup baby corn cobs, halved
3 tbsp fresh coriander (cilantro), roughly chopped
100g/3½ oz cherry tomatoes, halved
225 g/8 oz fan-tail prawns (shrimp)

1 Place the tamarind paste, chillies, garlic, ginger, fish sauce, sugar, lime leaves and stock in a large preheated wok. Bring to the boil, stirring constantly.

2 Reduce the heat and add the carrot, sweet potato and baby corn to the mixture in the wok.

3 Leave the soup to simmer, uncovered, for about 10 minutes, or until the vegetables are just tender.

4 Stir the coriander, cherry tomatoes and prawns (shrimp) into the soup and heat through for 5 minutes.

5 Transfer the soup to warm serving bowls and serve hot.

COOK'S TIP

Baby corn cobs have a sweet fragrance and flavour. They are available both fresh and canned.

COOK'S TIP

Thai ginger or galangal is a member of the ginger family, but it is yellow in colour with pink sprouts. The flavour is aromatic and less pungent than ginger.

Vegetable Spring Rolls

Serves 4

INGREDIENTS

- 225 g/8 oz carrots
- 1 red (bell) pepper
- 1 tbsp sunflower oil, plus extra for frying
- 75 g/2¾ oz/¾ cup beansprouts
- finely grated zest and juice of 1 lime
- 1 red chilli, deseeded and very finely chopped
- 1 tbsp soy sauce
- ½ tsp arrowroot
- 2 tbsp chopped fresh coriander (cilantro)
- 8 sheets filo pastry
- 25 g/1 oz butter
- 2 tsp sesame oil

TO SERVE:

- chili sauce
- spring onion (scallion) tassels

1 Using a sharp knife, cut the carrots into thin sticks. Deseed the red (bell) pepper and cut into thin slices.

2 Heat the sunflower oil in a large preheated wok.

3 Add the carrot, red (bell) pepper and beansprouts and cook, stirring, for 2 minutes, or until softened. Remove the wok from the heat and toss in the lime zest and juice, and the red chilli.

4 Mix the soy sauce with the arrowroot. Stir the mixture into the wok, return to the heat and cook for 2 minutes or until the juices thicken. Add the coriander (cilantro) and mix well.

5 Lay the sheets of filo pastry out on a board. Melt the butter and sesame oil and brush each sheet with the mixture. Spoon a little of the vegetable filling at the top of each sheet, fold over each long side, and roll up.

6 Add a little oil to the wok and cook the spring rolls in batches, for 2–3 minutes, or until crisp and golden. Garnish with spring onion (scallion) tassels and serve hot with chilli dipping sauce.

COOK'S TIP

Use prepared spring roll skins available from Chinese supermarkets or health food shops instead of the filo pastry if liked.

1

4

5

Chinese Prawn (Shrimp) Salad

Serves 4

INGREDIENTS

250 g/9 oz fine egg noodles
3 tbsp sunflower oil
1 tbsp sesame oil
1 tbsp sesame seeds
150 g/$5\frac{1}{2}$ oz/$1\frac{1}{2}$ cups beansprouts
1 ripe mango, sliced
6 spring onions (scallions), sliced
75 g/$2\frac{3}{4}$ oz radish, sliced
350 g/12 oz peeled cooked prawns (shrimp)
2 tbsp light soy sauce
1 tbsp sherry

1 Place the egg noodles in a large bowl and pour over enough boiling water to cover. Leave to stand for 10 minutes.

2 Drain the noodles thoroughly and pat away any moisture with absorbent kitchen paper.

3 Heat the sunflower oil in a large wok. Add the noodles and stir-fry for 5 minutes, tossing frequently.

4 Remove the wok from the heat and add the sesame oil, sesame seeds and beansprouts, tossing to mix well.

5 In a separate bowl, mix together the sliced mango, spring onions (scallions), radish, prawns (shrimp), light soy sauce and sherry.

6 Toss the prawn (shrimp) mixture with the noodles or alternatively, arrange the noodles around the edge of a serving plate and pile the prawn (shrimp) mixture into the centre. Serve immediately.

VARIATION

If fresh mango is unavailable, use canned mango slices, rinsed and drained, instead.

Crispy Chilli & Peanut Prawns (Shrimp)

Serves 4

INGREDIENTS

450 g/1 lb king prawns (shrimp) (peeled apart from tail end)
3 tbsp crunchy peanut butter
1 tbsp chilli sauce
10 sheets filo pastry
25 g/1 oz butter, melted
50 g/1¾ oz fine egg noodles
oil, for frying

1 Using a sharp knife, make a small horizontal slit across the back of each prawn (shrimp). Press down on the prawns (shrimps) so that they lie flat.

2 Mix together the peanut butter and chilli sauce in a small bowl. Spread a little of the sauce on to each prawn (shrimp).

3 Cut each pastry sheet in half and brush with melted butter.

4 Wrap each prawn (shrimp) in a piece of pastry, tucking the edges under to fully enclose the prawn (shrimp).

5 Place the egg noodles in a bowl, pour over enough boiling water to cover and leave to stand for 5 minutes. Drain the noodles thoroughly. Use 2–3 cooked noodles to tie around each prawn (shrimp).

6 Heat the oil in a preheated wok. Cook the prawns (shrimp) for 3–4 minutes, or until golden and crispy.

7 Remove the prawns (shrimp) with a slotted spoon, transfer to absorbent kitchen paper and leave to drain. Transfer to serving plates and serve warm.

COOK'S TIP

When using filo pastry, keep any unused pastry covered to prevent it drying out and becoming brittle.

1

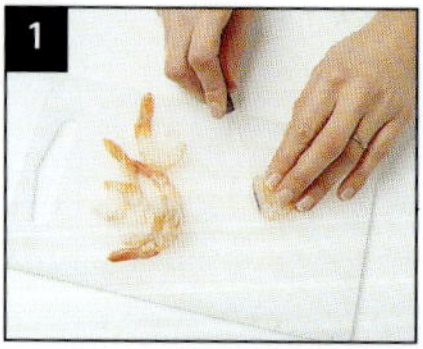

2

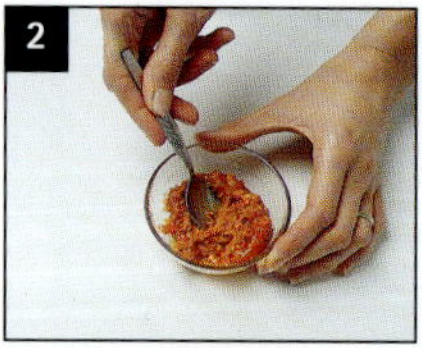

5

Stir-Fried Ginger Chicken

Serves 4

INGREDIENTS

2 tbsp sunflower oil
1 onion, sliced
175 g/6 oz carrots, cut into thin sticks
1 clove garlic, crushed
350 g/12 oz boneless skinless chicken breasts
2 tbsp fresh ginger, peeled and grated
1 tsp ground ginger
4 tbsp sweet sherry
1 tbsp tomato purée
1 tbsp demerara sugar
100 ml/3½ fl oz/⅓ cup orange juice
1 tsp cornflour (cornstarch)
1 orange, peeled and segmented
fresh snipped chives, to garnish

1 Heat the oil in a large preheated wok. Add the onion, carrots and garlic and stir-fry over a high heat for 3 minutes or until the vegetables begin to soften.

2 Using a sharp knife, slice the chicken into thin strips. Add the chicken to the wok together with the fresh ginger and ground ginger. Stir-fry for a further 10 minutes, or until the chicken is well cooked through and golden in colour.

3 Mix together the sherry, tomato purée, sugar, orange juice and cornflour (cornstarch) in a bowl. Stir the mixture into the wok and heat through until the mixture bubbles and the juices start to thicken.

4 Add the orange segments and carefully toss to mix.

5 Transfer the stir-fried chicken to warm serving bowls and garnish with freshly snipped chives. Serve immediately.

COOK'S TIP

Make sure that you do not continue cooking the dish once the orange segments have been added in step 4, otherwise they will break up.

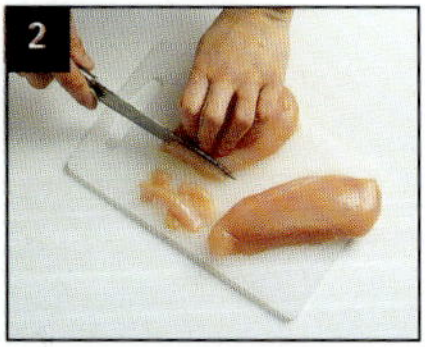

Coconut Chicken Curry

Serves 4

INGREDIENTS

- 2 tbsp sunflower oil or 25 g/1 oz ghee
- 450 g/1 lb boneless, skinless chicken thighs or breasts
- 150 g/5½ oz/1 cup okra
- 1 large onion, sliced
- 2 cloves garlic, crushed
- 3 tbsp mild curry paste
- 300 ml/½ pint/2¼ cups chicken stock
- 1 tbsp fresh lemon juice
- 100 g/3½ oz/½ cup creamed coconut
- 175 g/6 oz/1¼ cups fresh or canned pineapple, cubed
- 150 ml/¼ pint/⅔ cup thick, natural yogurt
- 2 tbsp chopped fresh coriander (cilantro)
- freshly boiled rice, to serve

TO GARNISH:

- lemon wedges
- fresh coriander (cilantro) sprigs

1 Heat the sunflower oil or ghee in a large preheated wok.

2 Using a sharp knife, cut the chicken into bite-sized pieces. Add the chicken to the wok and cook, stirring frequently, until evenly browned.

3 Using a sharp knife, trim the okra.

4 Add the onion, garlic and okra to the wok and cook for a further 2–3 minutes, stirring constantly.

5 Mix the curry paste with the chicken stock and lemon juice and pour over the mixture in the wok. Bring to the boil, cover and leave to simmer for 30 minutes.

6 Coarsley grate the creamed coconut, stir it into the curry and cook for about 5 minutes – the creamed coconut will help to thicken the juices.

7 Add the pineapple, yogurt and coriander (cilantro) and heat through for 2 minutes, stirring.

8 Garnish and serve hot with boiled rice.

COOK'S TIP

Score around the top of the okra with a knife before cooking to release the sticky glue-like substance which is bitter in taste.

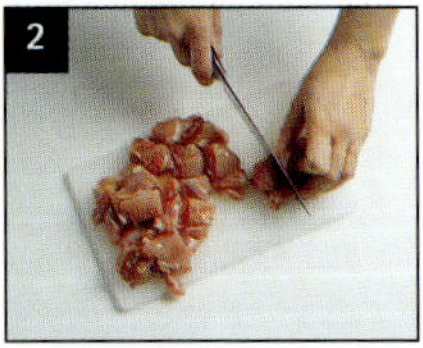

Thai Red Chicken with Cherry Tomatoes

Serves 4

INGREDIENTS

- 1 tbsp sunflower oil
- 450 g/1 lb boneless, skinless chicken
- 2 cloves garlic, crushed
- 2 tbsp Thai red curry paste
- 2 tbsp fresh grated galangal or root ginger
- 1 tbsp tamarind paste
- 4 lime leaves
- 225 g/8 oz sweet potato
- 600 ml/1 pint/2½ cups coconut milk
- 225 g/8 oz cherry tomatoes, halved
- 3 tbsp chopped fresh coriander (cilantro)
- cooked jasmine or Thai fragrant rice, to serve

1 Heat the sunflower oil in a large preheated wok.

2 Thinly slice the chicken. Add the chicken to the wok and stir-fry for 5 minutes.

3 Add the garlic, curry paste, galangal or root ginger, tamarind and lime leaves to the wok and stir-fry for 1 minute.

4 Using a sharp knife, peel and dice the sweet potato.

5 Add the coconut milk and sweet potato to the mixture in the wok and bring to the boil. Allow to bubble over a medium heat for 20 minutes, or until the juices start to thicken and reduce.

6 Add the cherry tomatoes and coriander (cilantro) to the curry and cook for a further 5 minutes, stirring occasionally. Transfer to serving plates and serve hot with cooked jasmine or Thai fragrant rice.

COOK'S TIP

Galangal is a spice very similar to ginger and is used to replace the latter in Thai cuisine. It can be bought fresh from Oriental food stores but is also available dried and as a powder. The fresh root, which is not as pungent as ginger, needs to be peeled before slicing.

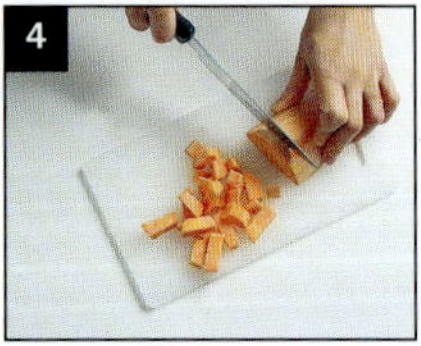

Peppered Chicken Stir-Fried with Sugar Snap Peas

Serves 4

INGREDIENTS

2 tbsp tomato ketchup
2 tbsp soy sauce
450 g/1 lb boneless, skinless chicken breasts
2 tbsp crushed mixed peppercorns
2 tbsp sunflower oil
1 red (bell) pepper
1 green (bell) pepper
175 g/6 oz/2½ cups sugar snap peas
2 tbsp oyster sauce

1 Mix the tomato ketchup with the soy sauce in a bowl.

2 Using a sharp knife, slice the chicken into thin strips. Toss the chicken in the tomato ketchup and soy sauce mixture.

3 Sprinkle the crushed peppercorns on to a plate. Dip the coated chicken in the peppercorns until evenly coated.

4 Heat the sunflower oil in a preheated wok.

5 Add the chicken to the wok and stir-fry for 5 minutes.

6 Deseed and slice the (bell) peppers.

7 Add the (bell) peppers to the wok together with the sugar snap peas and stir-fry for a further 5 minutes.

8 Add the oyster sauce and allow to bubble for 2 minutes. Transfer to serving bowls and serve immediately.

VARIATION

Use mangetout (snow peas) instead of sugar snap peas, if you prefer.

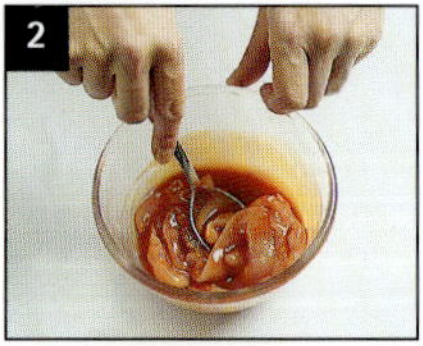

Stir-Fried Chicken with Cashew Nuts & Yellow Bean Sauce

Serves 4

INGREDIENTS

450 g/1 lb boneless chicken breasts
2 tbsp vegetable oil
1 red onion, sliced
175 g/6 oz/1½ cups flat mushrooms, sliced
100 g/3½ oz/⅓ cup cashew nuts
75 g/2¾ oz jar yellow bean sauce
fresh coriander (cilantro), to garnish
egg fried rice or plain boiled rice, to serve

1 Using a sharp knife, remove the excess skin from the chicken breasts if desired. Cut the chicken into small, bite-sized chunks.

2 Heat the vegetable oil in a preheated wok.

3 Add the chicken to the wok and stir-fry for 5 minutes.

4 Add the red onion and mushrooms to the wok and continue to stir fry for a further 5 minutes.

5 Place the cashew nuts on a baking tray (cookie sheet) and toast under a preheated medium grill (broiler) until just browning – this brings out their flavour.

6 Toss the toasted cashew nuts into the wok together with the yellow bean sauce. Allow the sauce to bubble for 2–3 minutes.

7 Transfer to warm serving bowls and garnish with fresh coriander (cilantro). Serve hot with egg fried rice or plain boiled rice.

COOK'S TIP

Chicken thighs could be used instead of the chicken breasts for a more economical dish.

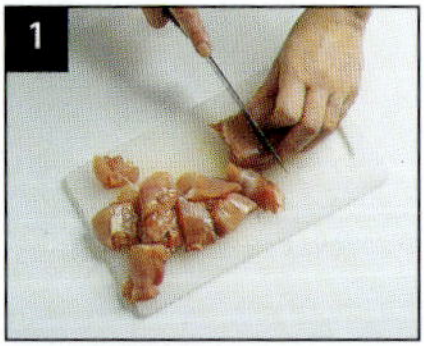

Duck with Baby Corn Cobs & Pineapple

Serves 4

INGREDIENTS

4 duck breasts
1 tsp Chinese five spice powder
1 tbsp cornflour (cornstarch)
1 tbsp chilli oil
225 g/8 oz baby onions, peeled
2 cloves garlic, crushed
100 g/3½ oz/1 cup baby corn cobs
175 g/6 oz/1¼ cups canned pineapple chunks
6 spring onions (scallions), sliced
100 g/3½ oz/1 cup beansprouts
2 tbsp plum sauce

1 Remove any skin from the duck breasts. Cut the duck breasts into thin slices.

2 Mix together the five spice powder and the cornflour (cornstarch) in a large bowl.

3 Toss the duck in the five spice powder and cornflour (cornstarch) mixture until well coated.

4 Heat the oil in a preheated wok. Stir-fry the duck for 10 minutes, or until just begining to crispen around the edges.

5 Remove the duck from the wok and set aside until required.

6 Add the onions and garlic to the wok and stir-fry for 5 minutes, or until the onions have softened.

7 Add the baby corn cobs to the wok and stir-fry for a further 5 minutes.

8 Add the pineapple, spring onions (scallions) and beansprouts and stir-fry for 3–4 minutes. Stir in the plum sauce.

9 Return the cooked duck to the wok and toss until well mixed. Transfer to warm serving dishes and serve hot.

COOK'S TIP

Buy pineapple chunks in natural juice rather than syrup for a fresher flavour. If you can only obtain pineapple in syrup, rinse it in cold water and drain thoroughly before using.

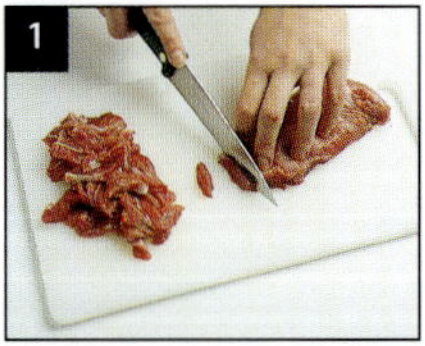

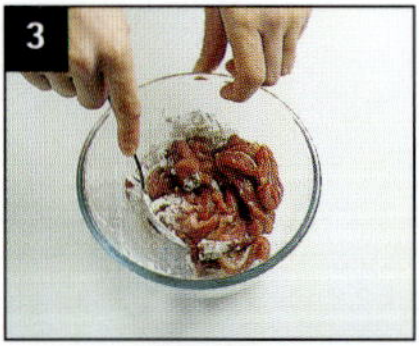

Stir-Fried Turkey with Cranberry Glaze

Serves 2–3

INGREDIENTS

1 turkey breast
2 tbsp sunflower oil
15 g/½ oz/2 tbsp stem ginger
50 g/1¾ oz/½ cup fresh or frozen cranberries
100 g/3½ oz/¼ cup canned chestnuts
4 tbsp cranberry sauce
3 tbsp light soy sauce
salt and pepper

1 Remove any skin from the turkey breast. Using a sharp knife, thinly slice the turkey breast.

2 Heat the oil in a large preheated wok.

3 Add the turkey to the wok and stir-fry for 5 minutes, or until cooked through.

4 Using a sharp knife, finely chop the stem ginger.

5 Add the ginger and the cranberries to the wok and stir-fry for 2–3 minutes or until the cranberries have softened.

6 Add the chestnuts, cranberry sauce and soy sauce, season to taste with salt and pepper and allow to bubble for 2–3 minutes.

7 Transfer to warm serving dishes and serve immediately.

COOK'S TIP

If you wish, use a turkey escalope instead of the breast for really tender, lean meat.

COOK'S TIP

It is very important that the wok is very hot before you stir-fry. Test by holding your hand flat about 7.5 cm/3 inches above the base of the interior – you should be able to feel the heat radiating from it.

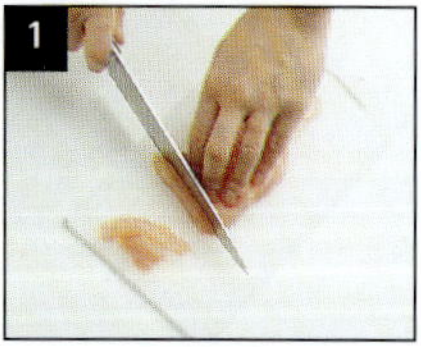
1

3

4

Stir-Fried Beef & Vegetables with Sherry & Soy Sauce

Serves 4

INGREDIENTS

2 tbsp sunflower oil
350 g/12 oz fillet of beef, sliced
1 red onion, sliced
175 g/6 oz courgettes (zucchini), sliced diagonally
175 g/6 oz carrots, thinly sliced
1 red (bell) pepper, deseeded and sliced
1 small head Chinese leaves, shredded
150 g/5½ oz/1½ cups beansprouts
225 g/8 oz can bamboo shoots, drained
150 g/5½ oz/½ cup cashew nuts, toasted

SAUCE:
3 tbsp medium sherry
3 tbsp light soy sauce
1 tsp ground ginger
1 clove garlic, crushed
1 tsp cornflour (cornstarch)
1 tbsp tomato purée

1 Heat the sunflower oil in a large preheated wok.

2 Add the beef and onion to the wok and stir-fry for 4–5 minutes or until the onion begins to soften and the meat is just browning.

3 Using a sharp knife, trim the courgette (zucchini) and slice diagonally.

4 Add the carrots, (bell) pepper, and courgettes (zucchini) and stir-fry for 5 minutes.

5 Toss in the Chinese leaves, beansprouts and bamboo shoots and heat through for 2–3 minutes, or until the leaves are just beginning to wilt.

6 Scatter the cashew nuts over the stir-fry.

7 To make the sauce, mix together the sherry, soy sauce, ground ginger, garlic, cornflour (cornstarch) and tomato purée. Pour the sauce over the stir-fry and toss until well combined. Allow the sauce to bubble for 2–3 minutes or until the juices start to thicken.

8 Transfer to warm serving dishes and serve at once.

2

3

4

Sweet Potato Stir-Fry with Coconut Beef

Serves 4

INGREDIENTS

- 2 tbsp vegetable oil
- 350 g/12 oz rump steak
- 2 cloves garlic
- 1 onion, sliced
- 350 g/12 oz sweet potato
- 2 tbsp Thai red curry paste
- 300 ml/½ pint/1¼ cups coconut milk
- 3 limes leaves
- cooked jasmine rice, to serve

1 Heat the vegetable oil in a large preheated wok.

2 Using a sharp knife, thinly slice the beef. Add the beef to the wok and stir-fry for about 2 minutes or until sealed on all sides.

3 Add the garlic and the onion to the wok and stir-fry for a further 2 minutes.

4 Using a sharp knife, peel and dice the sweet potato.

5 Add the sweet potato to the wok with the curry paste, coconut milk and lime leaves and bring to a rapid boil. Reduce the heat, cover and leave to simmer for about 15 minutes or until the potatoes are tender.

6 Remove the lime leaves and transfer the stir-fry to warm serving bowls. Serve hot with cooked jasmine rice.

COOK'S TIP

If you cannot obtain lime leaves, use grated lime zest instead.

COOK'S TIP

There are two basic curry pastes used in Thai cuisine – red and green, depending on whether they are made from red or green chillies.

Pork Fillet Stir-Fry with Crunchy Satay Sauce

Serves 4

INGREDIENTS

150 g/5½ oz carrots
2 tbsp sunflower oil
350 g/12 oz pork neck fillet, thinly sliced
1 onion, sliced
2 cloves garlic, crushed
1 yellow (bell) pepper, deseeded and sliced
150 g/5½ oz/2⅓ cups mangetout (snow peas)
75 g/3 oz/1½ cups fine asparagus
chopped salted peanuts, to serve

SATAY SAUCE:
6 tbsp crunchy peanut butter
6 tbsp coconut milk
1 tsp chilli flakes
1 clove garlic, crushed
1 tsp tomato purée

1 Using a sharp knife, slice the carrots into thin sticks.

2 Heat the oil in a large wok. Add the pork, onion and garlic and stir-fry for 5 minutes or until the lamb is cooked through.

3 Add the carrots, (bell) pepper, mangetout (snow peas) and asparagus to the wok and stir-fry for 5 minutes.

4 To make the satay sauce, place the peanut butter, coconut milk, chilli flakes, garlic and tomato purée in a small pan and heat gently, stirring, until well combined.

5 Transfer the stir-fry to warm serving plates. Spoon the satay sauce over the stir-fry and scatter with chopped peanuts. Serve immediately.

COOK'S TIP

Cook the sauce just before serving as it tends to thicken very quickly and will not be spoonable if you cook it too far in advance.

Chinese Five Spice Crispy Pork with Egg Fried Rice

Serves 4

INGREDIENTS

275 g/9½ oz/1¼ cups long-grain white rice
600 ml/1 pint/2½ cups cold water
350 g/12 oz pork tenderloin
2 tsp Chinese five spice powder
25 g/1 oz/4 tbsp cornflour (cornstarch)
3 large eggs, beaten
25 g/1 oz/2 tbsp demerara sugar
2 tbsp sunflower oil
1 onion
2 cloves garlic, crushed
100 g/3½ oz carrots, diced
1 red (bell) pepper, deseeded and diced
100 g/3½ oz/¾ cup peas
15 g/1 oz/2 tbsp butter
salt and pepper

1 Rinse the rice under cold running water. Place the rice in a large saucepan, add the cold water and a pinch of salt. Bring to the boil, cover, then reduce the heat and leave to simmer for about 9 minutes, or until all of the liquid has been absorbed and the rice is tender.

2 Meanwhile, slice the pork tenderloin into very thin pieces, using a sharp knife. Set aside until required.

3 Whisk together the five spice powder, cornflour (cornstarch), 1 egg and the demerara sugar. Toss the pork in the mixture until coated.

4 Heat the oil in a large wok. Add the pork and cook over a high heat until the pork is cooked through and crispy. Remove the pork from the wok with a slotted spoon and set aside.

5 Using a sharp knife, cut the onion into dice.

6 Add the onion, garlic, carrots, (bell) pepper and peas to the wok and stir-fry for 5 minutes.

7 Return the pork to the wok together with the cooked rice and stir-fry for 5 minutes.

8 Heat the butter in a frying pan (skillet). Add the remaining beaten eggs and cook until set. Turn out on to a clean board and slice thinly. Toss the strips of egg into the rice mixture and serve.

Stir-Fried Lamb with Black Bean Sauce & Mixed (Bell) Peppers

Serves 4

INGREDIENTS

- 450 g/1 lb lamb neck fillet or boneless leg of lamb chops
- 1 egg white, lightly beaten
- 25 g/1 oz/4 tbsp cornflour (cornstarch)
- 1 tsp Chinese five spice powder
- 3 tbsp sunflower oil
- 1 red onion
- 1 red (bell) pepper, deseeded and sliced
- 1 green (bell) pepper, deseeded and sliced
- 1 yellow or orange (bell) pepper, deseeded and sliced
- 5 tbsp black bean sauce
- boiled rice or noodles, to serve

1 Using a sharp knife, slice the lamb into very thin strips.

2 Mix the egg white, cornflour (cornstarch) and Chinese five spice powder together in a large bowl. Toss the lamb strips in the mixture until evenly coated.

3 Heat the oil in a large preheated wok. Add the lamb and stir-fry over a high heat for 5 minutes or until the edges begin to crispen.

4 Using a sharp knife, slice the red onion. Add the onion and (bell) pepper slices to the wok and stir-fry for 5–6 minutes, or until the vegetables just begin to soften.

5 Stir the black bean sauce into the mixture in the wok and heat through.

6 Transfer the lamb and sauce to warm serving plates and serve hot with freshly boiled rice or noodles.

COOK'S TIP

Take care when frying the lamb as the cornflour (cornstarch) mixture may cause it to stick to the wok. Move the lamb around the wok constantly during stir-frying.

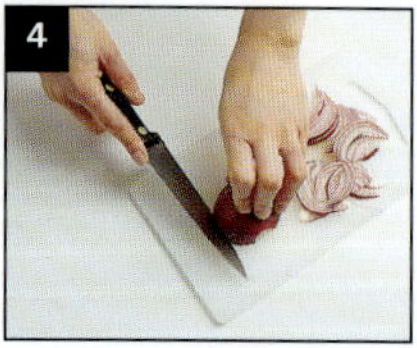

Curried Stir-Fried Lamb with Diced Potatoes

Serves 4

INGREDIENTS

450 g/1 lb potatoes, diced
450 g/1 lb lean lamb, cubed
2 tbsp medium hot curry paste
3 tbsp sunflower oil
1 onion, sliced
1 aubergine (eggplant), diced
2 cloves garlic, crushed
1 tbsp grated fresh root ginger
150 ml/5 fl oz/$^{2}/_{3}$ cup lamb or beef stock
2 tbsp chopped fresh coriander (cilantro)

1 Bring a large saucepan of lightly salted water to the boil. Add the potatoes and cook for 10 minutes. Remove the potatoes from the saucepan with a slotted spoon and drain thoroughly.

2 Meanwhile, place the lamb in a large mixing bowl. Add the curry paste and mix until well combined.

3 Heat the sunflower oil in a large preheated wok.

4 Add the onion, aubergine (eggplant), garlic and ginger to the wok and stir-fry for about 5 minutes.

5 Add the lamb to the wok and stir-fry for a further 5 minutes.

6 Add the stock and cooked potatoes to the wok, bring to the boil and leave to simmer for 30 minutes, or until the lamb is tender and completely cooked through.

7 Transfer the stir-fry to warm serving dishes and scatter with chopped fresh coriander (cilantro). Serve immediately.

COOK'S TIP

The wok is an ancient Chinese invention, the name coming from the Cantonese, meaning a 'cooking vessel'.

2

4

5

Stir-Fried Salmon with Pineapple

Serves 4

INGREDIENTS

100 g/3¾ oz/1 cup baby corn cobs, halved
2 tbsp sunflower oil
1 red onion, sliced
1 orange (bell) pepper, deseeded and sliced
1 green (bell) pepper, deseeded and sliced
450 g/1 lb salmon fillet, skin removed
1 tbsp paprika
225 g/8 oz can cubed pineapple, drained
100 g/3½ oz/1 cup beansprouts
2 tbsp tomato ketchup
2 tbsp soy sauce
2 tbsp medium sherry
1 tsp cornflour (cornstarch)

1 Using a sharp knife, cut the baby corn cobs in half.

2 Heat the sunflower oil in a large preheated wok. Add the onion, (bell) peppers and baby corn cobs to the wok and stir-fry for 5 minutes.

3 Rinse the salmon fillet under cold running water and pat dry with absorbent kitchen paper.

4 Cut the salmon flesh into thin strips and place in a large bowl. Sprinkle with the paprika and toss until well coated.

5 Add the salmon to the wok together with the pineapple and stir-fry for a further 2–3 minutes or until the fish is tender.

6 Add the beansprouts to the wok and toss well.

7 Mix together the tomato ketchup, soy sauce, sherry and cornflour (cornstarch). Add the mixture to the wok and cook until the juices start to thicken. Transfer to warm serving plates and serve immediately.

VARIATION

You can use trout fillets instead of the salmon as an alternative, if you prefer.

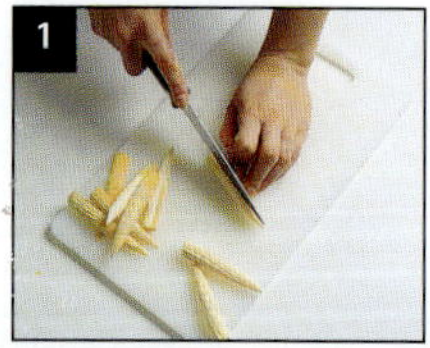

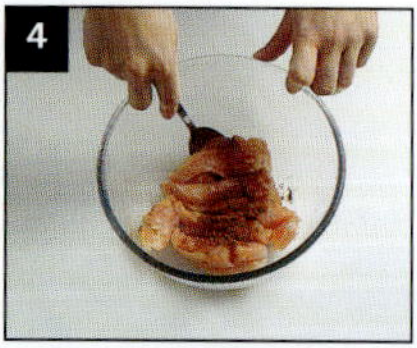

Tuna & Vegetable Stir-Fry

Serves 4

INGREDIENTS

225 g/8 oz carrots
2 tbsp corn oil
1 onion, sliced
175 g/6 oz/2½ cups mangetout (snow peas)
175 g/6 oz/1¾ cups baby corn cobs, halved
450 g/1 lb fresh tuna
2 tbsp fish sauce
15 g/½ oz/1 tbsp palm sugar
finely grated zest and juice of 1 orange
2 tbsp sherry
1 tsp cornflour (cornstarch)
rice or noodles, to serve

1 Using a sharp knife, cut the carrots into thin sticks.

2 Heat the corn oil in a large preheated wok.

3 Add the onion, carrots, mangetout (snow peas) and baby corn cobs to the wok and stir-fry for 5 minutes.

4 Using a sharp knife, thinly slice the tuna.

5 Add the tuna to the wok and stir-fry for 2–3 minutes, or until the tuna turns opaque.

6 Mix together the fish sauce, palm sugar, orange zest and juice, sherry and cornflour (cornstarch).

7 Pour the mixture over the tuna and vegetables and cook for 2 minutes, or until the juices thicken. Serve with rice or noodles.

VARIATION

Try using swordfish steaks instead of the tuna. Swordfish steaks are now widely available and are similar in texture to tuna.

COOK'S TIP

Palm sugar is a thick, coarse brown sugar that has a slightly caramel taste. It is sold in round cakes or in small, round, flat containers.

1
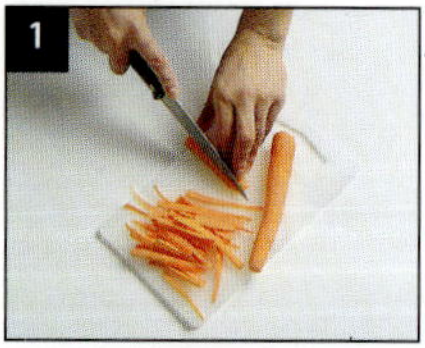

3

4
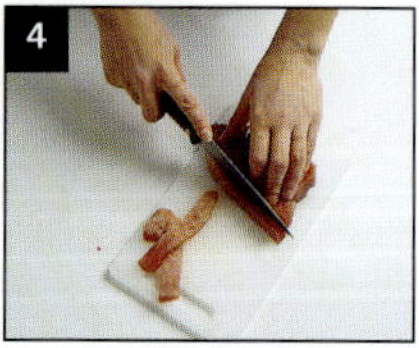

Stir-Fried Cod with Mango

Serves 4

INGREDIENTS

175 g/6 oz carrots
2 tbsp vegetable oil
1 red onion, sliced
1 red (bell) pepper, deseeded and sliced
1 green (bell) pepper, deseeded and sliced
450 g/1 lb skinless cod fillet
1 ripe mango
1 tsp cornflour (cornstarch)
1 tbsp soy sauce
100 ml/3½ fl oz/1⅓ cup tropical fruit juice
1 tbsp lime juice
1 tbsp chopped coriander (cilantro)

1 Using a sharp knife, slice the carrots into thin sticks.

2 Heat the vegetable oil in a preheated wok.

3 Add the onions, carrots and (bell) peppers to the wok and stir-fry for 5 minutes.

4 Using a sharp knife, cut the cod into small cubes.

5 Peel the mango, then carefully remove the flesh from the centre stone. Cut the flesh into thin slices.

6 Add the cod and mango to the wok and stir-fry for a further 4–5 minutes, or until the fish is cooked through. Do not stir the mixture too much or you may break the fish up.

7 Mix the cornflour (cornstarch), soy sauce, fruit juice and lime juice in a small bowl.

8 Pour the cornflour (cornstarch) mixture over the stir-fry and allow the mixture to bubble and the juices to thicken. Scatter with coriander (cilantro) and serve immediately.

VARIATION

You can use paw-paw (papaya) as an alternative to the mango, if you prefer.

1

5

7

Mussels in Black Bean Sauce with Spinach

Serves 4

INGREDIENTS

- 350 g/12 oz leeks
- 350 g/12 oz cooked green-lipped mussels (shelled)
- 1 tsp cumin seeds
- 2 tbsp vegetable oil
- 2 cloves garlic, crushed
- 1 red (bell) pepper, deseeded and sliced
- 50 g/1¾ oz/¾ cup canned bamboo shoots, drained
- 175 g/6 oz baby spinach
- 160 g/5¾ oz jar black bean sauce

1 Using a sharp knife, trim the leeks and shred them.

2 Place the mussels in a large bowl, sprinkle with the cumin seeds and toss well to coat all over.

3 Heat the vegetable oil in a large preheated wok.

4 Add the leeks, garlic and red (bell) pepper to the wok and stir-fry for 5 minutes, or until the vegetables are tender.

5 Add the bamboo shoots, baby spinach leaves and cooked green-lipped mussels to the wok and stir-fry for about 2 minutes.

6 Pour the black bean sauce over the ingredients in the wok, toss well to coat all over and leave to simmer for a few seconds, stirring occasionally.

7 Transfer the stir-fry to warm serving bowls and serve immediately.

COOK'S TIP

If the green-lipped mussels are not available they can be bought shelled in cans and jars from most large supermarkets.

1

4

5

Chinese Vegetable Rice

Serves 4

INGREDIENTS

350 g/12 oz/1¾ cups long-grain white rice
1 tsp turmeric
2 tbsp sunflower oil
225 g/8 oz courgettes (zucchini), sliced
1 red (bell) pepper, deseeded and sliced
1 green (bell) pepper, deseeded and sliced
1 green chilli, deseeded and finely chopped
1 medium carrot, coarsley grated
150 g/5½ oz/1½ cups beansprouts
6 spring onions (scallions), sliced, plus extra to garnish
2 tbsp soy sauce

1 Place the rice and turmeric in a saucepan of lightly salted water and bring to the boil. Reduce the heat and leave to simmer until the rice is just tender. Drain the rice thoroughly and press out any excess water with a sheet of double thickness kitchen paper.

2 Heat the sunflower oil in a large preheated wok.

3 Add the courgettes (zucchini) to the wok and stir-fry for about 2 minutes.

4 Add the (bell) peppers and chilli to the wok and stir-fry for 2–3 minutes.

5 Add the cooked rice to the mixture in the wok, a little at a time, tossing well after each addition.

6 Add the carrots, beansprouts and spring onions (scallions) to the wok and stir-fry for a further 2 minutes. Drizzle with soy sauce and serve at once, garnished with extra spring onions (scallions), if desired.

VARIATION

For real luxury, add a few saffron strands infused in boiling water instead of the turmeric.

1

4

5

Vegetable Stir-Fry with Hoisin Sauce

Serves 4

INGREDIENTS

2 tbsp sunflower oil
1 red onion, sliced
100 g/3½ oz carrots, sliced
1 yellow (bell) pepper, deseeded and diced
50 g/1¾ oz/1 cup cooked brown rice
175 g/6 oz mangetout (snow peas)
175 g/6 oz/1½ cups beansprouts
4 tbsp hoisin sauce
1 tbsp snipped fresh chives

1 Heat the sunflower oil in a large preheated wok.

2 Add the red onion slices, carrots and yellow (bell) pepper to the wok and stir-fry for about 3 minutes.

3 Add the cooked brown rice, mangetout (snow peas) and beansprouts to the mixture in the wok and stir-fry for a further 2 minutes.

4 Stir the hoisin sauce into the vegetables and mix until well combined and completely heated through.

5 Transfer to warm serving dishes and scatter with the snipped fresh chives. Serve immediately.

COOK'S TIP

Hoisin sauce is a dark brown, reddish sauce made from soy beans, garlic, chilli and various other spices, and is commonly used in Chinese cookery. It may also be used as a dipping sauce.

VARIATION

Almost any vegetables could be used in this dish: other good choices would be broccoli florets, baby corn cobs, green peas, Chinese leaves and young spinach leaves. Either white or black (oyster) mushrooms can also be used to give a greater diversity of textures. In addition, make sure that there is a good variety of colour in this dish.

Vegetable Stir-Fry

Serves 4

INGREDIENTS

3 tbsp olive oil
8 baby onions, halved
1 aubergine (eggplant), cubed
225 g/8 oz courgettes (zucchini), sliced
225 g/8 oz open-cap mushrooms, halved
2 cloves garlic, crushed
400 g/14 oz can chopped tomatoes
2 tbsp sundried tomato purée
freshly ground black pepper
fresh basil leaves, to garnish

1 Heat the olive oil in a large preheated wok.

2 Add the baby onions and aubergine (eggplant) to the wok and stir-fry for 5 minutes, or until the vegetables are golden and just beginning to soften.

3 Add the courgettes (zucchini), mushrooms, garlic, tomatoes and tomato purée to the wok and stir-fry for about 5 minutes. Reduce the heat and leave to simmer for 10 minutes, or until the vegetables are tender.

4 Season with freshly ground black pepper and scatter with fresh basil leaves. Serve immediately.

VARIATION

If you want to serve this as a vegetarian main meal, add cubed tofu (bean curd) in step 3.

COOK'S TIP

Wok cooking is an excellent means of cooking for vegetarians as it is a quick and easy way of serving up delicious dishes of crisp, tasty vegetables. All ingredients should be cut into uniform sizes with as many cut surfaces exposed as possible for quick cooking.

Coconut Rice

Serves 4

INGREDIENTS

275 g/9½ oz long-grain white rice
600 ml/1 pint/2½ cups water
½ tsp salt
100 ml/3½ fl oz/⅓ cup coconut milk
25 g/1 oz/¼ cup desiccated (shredded) coconut

1 Rinse the rice thoroughly under cold running water until the water runs clear.

2 Drain the rice thoroughly in a sieve set over a large bowl.

3 Place the rice in a wok with 600 ml/1 pint/2½ cups water.

4 Add the salt and coconut milk to the wok and bring to the boil. Cover the wok, reduce the heat and leave to simmer for 10 minutes.

5 Remove the lid from the wok and fluff up the rice with a fork – all of the liquid should be absorbed and the rice grains should be tender.

6 Spoon the coconut rice into a warm serving bowl and scatter with the desiccated (shredded) coconut. Serve immediately.

COOK'S TIP

The rice is rinsed under cold running water to remove some of the starch and to prevent the grains from sticking together.

COOK'S TIP

Coconut milk is not the liquid found inside coconuts – that is called coconut water. Coconut milk is made from the white coconut flesh soaked in water and milk and then squeezed to extract all of the flavour. You can make your own or buy it in cans.

2

3

5

Chicken Chow Mein

Serves 4

INGREDIENTS

250 g/9 oz packet of medium egg noodles
2 tbsp sunflower oil
275 g/9½ oz cooked chicken breasts, shredded
1 clove garlic, finely chopped
1 red (bell) pepper, deseeded and thinly sliced
100 g/3½ oz shiitake mushrooms, sliced
6 spring onions (scallions), sliced
100 g/3½ oz/1 cup beansprouts
3 tbsp soy sauce
1 tbsp sesame oil

1 Place the egg noodles in a large bowl or dish and break them up slightly.

2 Pour enough boiling water over the noodles to cover and leave to stand whilst preparing the other ingredients.

3 Heat the sunflower oil in a large preheated wok.

4 Add the shredded chicken, finely chopped garlic, (bell) pepper slices, mushrooms, spring onions (scallions) and beansprouts to the wok and stir-fry for about 5 minutes.

5 Drain the noodles thoroughly. Add the noodles to the wok, toss well and stir-fry for a further 5 minutes.

6 Drizzle the soy sauce and sesame oil over the chow mein and toss until well combined.

7 Transfer the chicken chow mein to warm serving bowls and serve immediately.

VARIATION

You can make the chow mein with a selection of vegetables for a vegetarian dish, if you prefer.

1

4

5

Egg Noodles with Chicken & Oyster Sauce

Serves 4

INGREDIENTS

250 g/9 oz egg noodles
450 g/1 lb chicken thighs
2 tbsp groundnut oil
100 g/3½ oz carrots, sliced
3 tbsp oyster sauce
2 eggs
3 tbsp cold water

1 Place the egg noodles in a large bowl or dish. Pour enough boiling water over the noodles to cover and leave to stand for 10 minutes.

2 Meanwhile, remove the skin from the chicken thighs. Cut the chicken flesh into small pieces, using a sharp knife.

3 Heat the groundnut oil in a large preheated wok.

4 Add the pieces of chicken and the carrot slices to the wok and stir-fry the mixture for about 5 minutes.

5 Drain the noodles thoroughly. Add the noodles to the wok and stir-fry for a further 2–3 minutes or until the noodles are heated through.

6 Beat together the oyster sauce, eggs and 3 tablespoons of cold water. Drizzle the mixture over the noodles and stir-fry for a further 2–3 minutes or until the eggs set. Transfer to warm serving bowls and serve hot.

VARIATION

Flavour the eggs with soy sauce or hoisin sauce as an alternative to the oyster sauce, if you prefer.

1

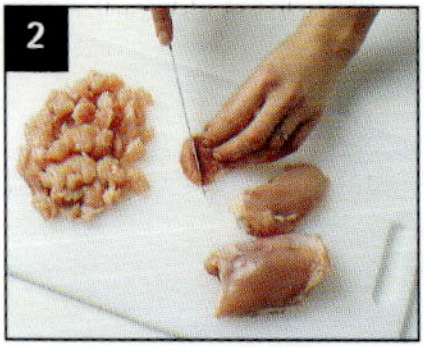
2

4

Ginger Chilli Beef with Crispy Noodles

Serves 4

INGREDIENTS

225 g/8 oz medium egg noodles
350 g/12 oz beef fillet
2 tbsp sunflower oil
1 tsp ground ginger
1 clove garlic, crushed
1 red chilli, deseeded and very finely chopped
100 g/3½ oz carrots, cut into thin sticks
6 spring onions (scallions), sliced
2 tbsp lime marmalade
2 tbsp soy sauce
oil, for frying

1 Place the noodles in a large dish or bowl. Pour over enough boiling water to cover the noodles and leave to stand for about 10 minutes while you stir-fry the rest of the ingredients.

2 Using a sharp knife, thinly slice the beef.

3 Heat the sunflower oil in a large preheated wok.

4 Add the beef and ginger to the wok and stir-fry for about 5 minutes.

5 Add the garlic, chilli, carrots and spring onions (scallions) to the wok and stir-fry for a further 2–3 minutes.

6 Add the lime marmalade and soy sauce to the wok and allow to bubble for 2 minutes. Remove the chilli beef and ginger mixture, set aside and keep warm.

7 Heat the oil for frying in the wok.

8 Drain the noodles thoroughly and pat dry with absorbent kitchen paper. Carefully lower the noodles into the hot oil and cook for 2–3 minutes or until crispy. Drain the noodles on absorbent kitchen paper.

9 Divide the noodles between 4 serving plates and top with the chilli beef and ginger mixture. Serve immediately.

VARIATION

Use pork or chicken instead of the beef, if you prefer.

2

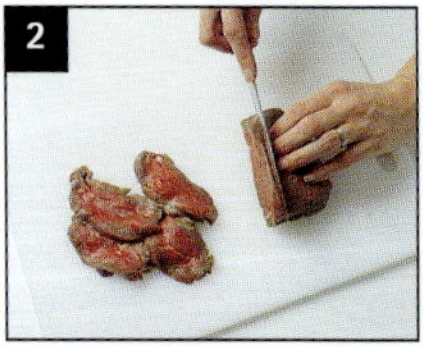

6

8

Twice-Cooked Lamb with Noodles

Serves 4

INGREDIENTS

250 g/9 oz packet egg noodles
450 g/1 lb lamb loin fillet, thinly sliced
2 tbsp soy sauce
2 tbsp sunflower oil
2 cloves garlic, crushed
1 tbsp caster (superfine) sugar
2 tbsp oyster sauce
175 g/6 oz baby spinach

1 Place the egg noodles in a large bowl and cover with boiling water. Leave to soak for about 10 minutes.

2 Bring a large saucepan of water to the boil. Add the lamb and cook for 5 minutes. Drain thoroughly.

3 Place the slices of lamb in a bowl and mix with the soy sauce and 1 tablespoon of the sunflower oil.

4 Heat the remaining sunflower oil in a large preheated wok.

5 Add the marinated lamb and garlic to the wok and stir-fry for about 5 minutes or until just beginning to brown.

6 Add the caster (superfine) sugar and oyster sauce to the wok and stir to combine.

7 Drain the noodles thoroughly. Add the noodles to the wok and stir-fry for a further 5 minutes.

8 Add the spinach to the wok and cook for 1 minute or until the leaves just wilt. Transfer the lamb and noodles to serving bowls and serve hot.

COOK'S TIP

If using dried noodles, follow the instructions on the packet as they require less soaking.

Stir-Fried (Bell) Pepper Trio with Chestnuts & Garlic

Serves 4

INGREDIENTS

225 g/8 oz leeks
oil, for deep-frying
3 tbsp groundnut oil
1 yellow (bell) pepper, deseeded and diced
1 green (bell) pepper, deseeded and diced
1 red (bell) pepper, deseeded and diced
200 g/7 oz can water chestnuts, drained and sliced
2 cloves garlic, crushed
3 tbsp light soy sauce

1 To make the garnish, finely slice the leeks into thin strips, using a sharp knife.

2 Heat the oil for deep-frying in a wok and cook the leeks for 2–3 minute, or until crispy. Set the crispy leeks aside until required.

3 Heat the 3 tablespoons of groundnut oil in the wok.

4 Add the (bell) peppers to the wok and stir-fry over a high heat for about 5 minutes, or until they are just beginning to brown at the edges and to soften.

5 Add the sliced water chestnuts, garlic and light soy sauce to the wok and stir-fry all of the vegetables for a further 2–3 minutes.

6 Spoon the (bell) pepper stir-fry on to warm serving plates.

7 Garnish the stir-fry with the crispy leeks.

VARIATION

Add 1 tbsp of hoisin sauce with the soy sauce in step 5 for extra flavour and spice.

1

4

5

Fried Fish with Coconut & Basil

Serves 4

INGREDIENTS

2 tbsp vegetable oil
450 g/1 lb skinless cod fillet
25 g/1 oz/¼ cup seasoned flour
1 clove garlic, crushed
2 tbsp red Thai curry paste
1 tbsp fish sauce
300 ml/½ pint/1¼ cups coconut milk
175 g/6 oz cherry tomatoes, halved
20 fresh basil leaves
fragrant rice, to serve

1 Heat the vegetable oil in a large preheated wok.

2 Using a sharp knife, cut the fish into large cubes, taking care to remove any bones with a pair of tweezers.

3 Place the seasoned flour in a bowl. Add the cubes of fish and mix until well coated.

4 Add the coated fish to the wok and stir-fry over a high heat for 3–4 minutes, or until the fish just begins to brown at the edges.

5 Mix together the garlic, curry paste, fish sauce and coconut milk in a bowl. Pour the mixture over the fish and bring to the boil.

6 Add the tomatoes to the mixture in the wok and leave to simmer for 5 minutes.

7 Roughly chop or tear the fresh basil leaves. Add the basil to the wok, stir carefully to combine, taking care not to break up the cubes of fish.

8 Transfer to serving plates and serve hot with fragrant rice.

COOK'S TIP

Take care not to overcook the dish once the tomatoes are added, otherwise they will break down and the skins will come away.

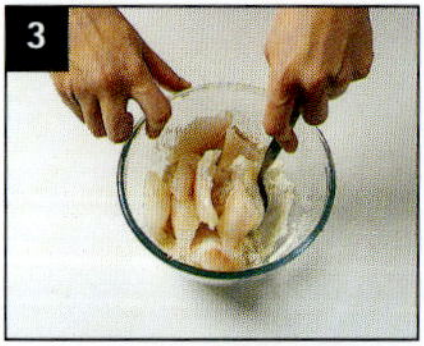

Garlic-Infused Lamb with Soy Sauce

Serves 4

INGREDIENTS

450 g/1 lb lamb loin fillet
2 cloves garlic
2 tbsp groundnut oil
3 tbsp dry sherry or rice wine
3 tbsp dark soy
1 tsp cornflour (cornstarch)
2 tbsp cold water
25 g/1 oz/2 tbsp butter

1 Using a sharp knife, make small slits in the flesh of the lamb.

2 Carefully peel the cloves of garlic and cut them into slices, using a sharp knife.

3 Push the slices of garlic into the slits in the lamb. Place the garlic-infused lamb in a shallow dish.

4 Drizzle 1 tablespoon each of the oil, sherry and soy sauce over the lamb, cover and leave to marinate for at least 1 hour, preferably overnight.

5 Using a sharp knife, thinly slice the marinated lamb.

6 Heat the remaining oil in a preheated wok. Add the lamb and stir-fry for 5 minutes.

7 Add the marinade juices and the remaining sherry and soy sauce to the wok and allow the juices to bubble for 5 minutes.

8 Mix the cornflour (cornstarch) with the cold water. Add the cornflour (cornstarch) mixture to the wok and cook, stirring occasionally, until the juices start to thicken.

9 Cut the butter into small pieces. Add the butter to the wok and stir until the butter melts. Transfer to serving dishes and serve immediately.

COOK'S TIP

Adding the butter at the end of the recipe gives a glossy, rich sauce which is ideal with the lamb.

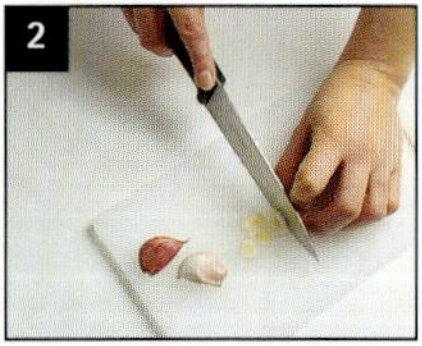

Twice-Cooked Pork with (Bell) Peppers

Serves 4

INGREDIENTS

15 g/½ oz Chinese dried mushrooms
450g/1 lb pork leg steaks
2 tbsp vegetable oil
1 onion, sliced
1 red (bell) pepper, deseeded and diced
1 green (bell) pepper, deseeded and diced
1 yellow (bell) pepper, deseeded and diced
4 tbsp oyster sauce

1 Place the mushrooms in a large bowl. Pour over enough boiling water to cover and leave to stand for 20 minutes.

2 Using a sharp knife, trim any excess fat from the pork steaks. Cut the pork into thin strips.

3 Bring a large saucepan of water to the boil. Add the pork to the boiling water and cook for 5 minutes.

4 Remove the pork from the pan with a slotted spoon and leave to drain thoroughly.

5 Heat the oil in a large preheated wok. Add the pork to the wok and stir-fry for about 5 minutes.

6 Remove the mushrooms from the water and leave to drain thoroughly. Roughly chop the mushrooms.

7 Add the mushrooms, onion and the (bell) peppers to the wok and stir-fry for 5 minutes.

8 Stir in the oyster sauce and cook for 2–3 minutes. Transfer to serving bowls and serve immediately.

VARIATION

Use open-cap mushrooms, sliced, instead of Chinese mushrooms, if you prefer.

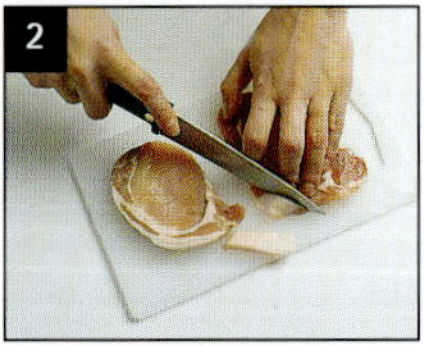
2

3

7

Stir-Fried Chicken with Chilli & Crispy Basil

Serves 4

INGREDIENTS

8 chicken drumsticks
2 tbsp soy sauce
1 tbsp sunflower oil
1 red chilli
100 g/3½ oz carrots, cut into thin sticks
6 celery stalks, cut into sticks
3 tbsp sweet chilli sauce
oil, for frying
about 50 fresh basil leaves

1 Remove the skin from the chicken drumsticks if desired. Make 3 slashes in each drumstick. Brush the drumsticks with the soy sauce.

2 Heat the oil in a preheated wok and fry the drumsticks for 20 minutes, turning frequently, until they are cooked through.

3 Deseed and finely chop the chilli. Add the chilli, carrots and celery to the wok and cook for a further 5 minutes. Stir in the chilli sauce, cover and allow to bubble gently whilst preparing the basil leaves.

4 Heat a little oil in a heavy based pan. Carefully add the basil leaves – stand well away from the pan and protect your hand with a tea towel (dish cloth) as they may spit a little. Cook for about 30 seconds or until they begin to curl up but not brown. Transfer to kitchen paper to drain.

5 Arrange the cooked chicken, vegetables and pan juices on to a warm serving plate and garnish with the deep-fried crispy basil leaves.

COOK'S TIP

Basil has a very strong flavour which is perfect with chicken and Chinese flavourings. You could use baby spinach instead of the basil, if you prefer.

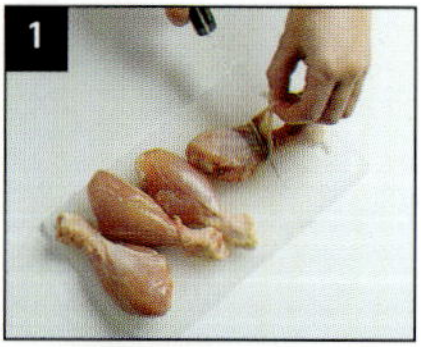
1

1

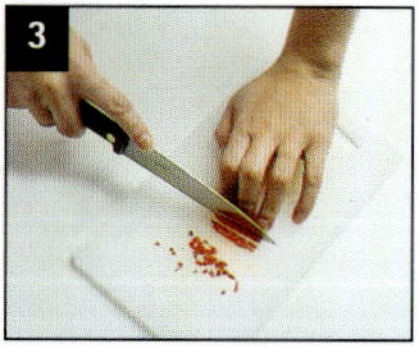
3

Stir-Fried Chicken with Cumin Seeds & Aubergine (Eggplant)

Serves 4

INGREDIENTS

5 tbsp sunflower oil
2 cloves garlic, crushed
1 tbsp cumin seeds
1 tbsp mild curry powder
1 tbsp paprika
450 g/1 lb boneless, skinless chicken breasts
1 large aubergine (eggplant), cubed
4 tomatoes, cut into quarters
100 ml/3½ fl oz/⅓ cup chicken stock
1 tbsp fresh lemon juice
½ tsp salt
150 ml/¼ pint/⅔ cup natural yogurt
1 tbsp chopped fresh mint

1 Heat 2 tablespoons of the sunflower oil in a large preheated wok.

2 Add the garlic, cumin seeds, curry powder and paprika to the wok and stir-fry for 1 minute.

3 Using a sharp knife, thinly slice the chicken breasts.

4 Add the rest of the oil to the wok and stir-fry the chicken for 5 minutes.

5 Add the aubergine (eggplant) cubes, tomatoes and chicken stock and bring to the boil. Reduce the heat and leave to simmer for about 20 minutes.

6 Stir in the lemon juice, salt and yogurt and cook over a gentle heat for a further 5 minutes, stirring occasionally.

7 Scatter with chopped fresh mint and transfer to serving bowls. Serve immediately.

COOK'S TIP

Once the yogurt has been added, do not boil the sauce as the yogurt will curdle.

This is a Parragon Book
First published in 2000

Parragon
Queen Street House
4 Queen Street
Bath BA1 1HE, UK

ISBN: 0-75253-620-6

Printed in China

Note

Cup measurements in this book are for American cups. Tablespoons are assumed to be 15 ml. Unless otherwise stated, milk is assumed to be full fat, eggs are medium and pepper is freshly ground black pepper.